Little Pebble™

Baby Animals and Their Homes

BABY ANIMALS In POUCHES

by Martha E. H. Rustad

CAPSTONE PRESS
a capstone imprint

Little Pebble is published by Capstone Press,
1710 Roe Crest Drive, North Mankato, Minnesota 56003
www.mycapstone.com

Library of Congress Cataloging-in-Publication Data
Names: Rustad, Martha E. H. (Martha Elizabeth Hillman), 1975- author.
Title: Baby animals in pouches / by Martha E.H. Rustad.
Description: North Mankato, Minnesota : Capstone Press, [2017] | Series:
  Little pebble. Baby animals and their homes | Audience: Ages 4-8.
  Audience: K to grade 3. | Includes bibliographical references and index.
Identifiers: LCCN 2016030474| ISBN 9781515738299 (library binding)
  ISBN 9781515738336 (pbk.) | ISBN 9781515738459 (ebook (pdf))
Subjects: LCSH: Marsupials—Infancy—Juvenile literature.
Classification: LCC QL737.M3 R87 2017 | DDC 599.2139—dc23
LC record available at https://lccn.loc.gov/2016030474

Editorial Credits
Carrie Braulick Sheely, editor; Juliette Peters, designer;
Tracey Engel, media researcher; Katy LaVigne, production specialist

Photo Credits
Alamy: Gerry Pearce, 11; Getty Images: Doug Cheeseman, 13, Roland Seitre/Minden Pictures,
7; Minden Pictures: S and D and K Maslowski, 20–21, Yva Momatiuk and John Eastcott, 17;
Nature Picture Library: Roland Seitre, 9; Science Source: ANT Photo Library, 15; Shutterstock:
Henri Faure, 3 Bottom Left, jeep2499, 19, K. A. Willis, Back Cover, Mikhail Blajenov, 5, optimarc,
Back Cover and Interior Design Element, SherrSS, 1 Bottom Left , sittipong, Back Cover Design
Element

Printed and bound in China.
007873

Table of Contents

Inside

Some baby animals
grow in pouches.
Pouches keep them safe.

Tiny hairless bandicoots
are born.
Mom has a pouch.
They settle in.

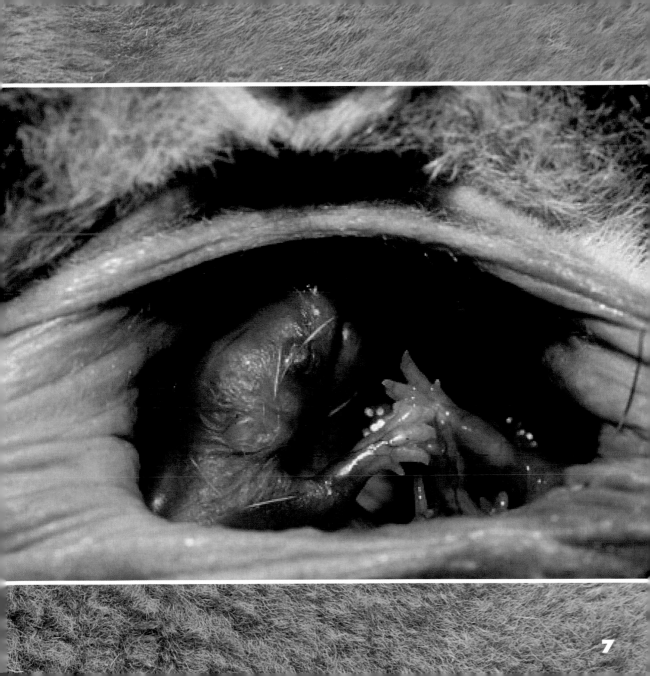

Baby Tasmanian devils eat. They drink milk from mom.

Bounce!

A wallaby looks out.

It is five months old.

A wombat lives below ground.

Her pouch faces backward.

Dirt stays out.

Her baby stays clean.

Outside

This mom rests with
her baby.
They are high in a tree.
They stay safe.

sugar gliders

Hop! A baby kangaroo plays.

It is tired.

It goes back in its pouch.

A koala is too big.

It moves to mom's back.

Baby opossums run.

Click!

Mom tells them

to stay close.

Glossary

bandicoot—a small Australian marsupial that has a pointy nose and a thin tail

pouch—a flap of skin on some female animals that holds their young; animals with pouches are called marsupials

wombat—an Australian marsupial that digs tunnels underground

Read More

Austen, Amy. *The Life Cycle of a Kangaroo.* Watch Them Grow! New York: PowerKids Press, 2016.

Marsh, Laura. *Koalas.* National Geographic Kids. Washington, D.C.: National Geographic, 2014.

Tatlock, Ann. *Opossums.* Backyard Jungle Safari. Kennett Square, Penn.: Purple Toad Publishing, Inc., 2015.

Internet Sites

FactHound offers a safe, fun way to find Internet sites related to this book. All of the sites on FactHound have been researched by our staff.

Here's all you do:
Visit *www.facthound.com*
Type in this code: 9781515738299

Check out projects, games and lots more at
www.capstonekids.com

Critical Thinking Using the Common Core

1. How does a mother wombat's pouch keep the baby clean? (Key Ideas and Details)

2. Some baby animals move from the pouch to their mothers' backs as they grow. How do you think this helps a baby animal stay safe? (Integration of Knowledge and Ideas)

Index